Migrations

ANNE CLUYSENAAR

INDEPENDENT INNOVATIVE INTERNATIONAL

Published by Cinnamon Press
Meirion House, Glan yr afon, Tanygrisiau
Blaenau Ffestiniog, Gwynedd, LL41 3SU
www.cinnamonpress.com

The right of Anne Cluysenaar to be identified as author of this
work has been asserted by her in accordance with the Copyright,
Designs and Patent Act, 1988. Copyright © 2011 Anne Cluysenaar
ISBN: 978-1-907090-41-7

British Library Cataloguing in Publication Data. A CIP record for
this book can be obtained from the British Library.

Designed and typeset in Palatino by Cinnamon Press.
Cover from original artwork © 'Tree Reflected in Water' by
rolfimages © agency: dreamstime.com
Cover design by Cottia Fortune-Wood.

Printed in Poland

Cinnamon Press is represented in the UK by Inpress Ltd
www.inpressbooks.co.uk and in Wales by the Welsh Books
Council www.cllc.org.uk.

The publisher acknowledges the support of the Welsh Books
Council.

Acknowledgements

The poems in MIGRATIONS have appeared in *Moment of Earth: Poems and Essays in Honour of Jeremy Hooker*, ed. Christopher Meredith (Celtic Studies 2007) and in the journals *Agenda – Irish Issue, Artemis, Modern Poetry in Translation - Green Issue, New Welsh Review, Orbis, Planet, Poetry Wales, Quattrocento, Scintilla, Temenos* and the following anthologies: *No Space But Their Own, Into The Further Reaches* and *The Lie of the Land*; also the *Open University Geological Society Newsletter, Second Light Newsletter* and *Ver Poets Competition booklet*.

The sequence 'Migrations' includes some poems originally published in my autobiographical sequence *Water to Breathe*, published in 2009, and I wish to thank Flarestack for permission to republish them here.

The sequence 'Clay' was awarded first prize in the Second Light Poetry Competition (long poem section), 2010, judge: Myra Schneider. It is with gratitude that I acknowledge the generosity of Penguin Publishers in allowing me to quote extensively, in 'Clay', from the 1999 Penguin Classics edition of *The Epic of Gilgamesh*, translated with an introduction by Andrew George (1999).

Contents

For Walt

'to be
just here'

On the Farm

Echo

for Gil Jackson-Hines

It's an exposed spot,
where we stand. From here
the forest can be heard: it shouts
but only if we shout first.

I expect you, step-grandson,
to delight in shouting, but
as I shout and the forest answers
you burst into tears, afraid.

Afraid perhaps of me,
of my voice magnified, thrown
down over both of us,
again and again, from that ridge?

Or of your silence, not
echoed, lost among trees,
among unseen trunks, branches,
roots gripping the stones.

What for me was poetic nicety
is for you the real terror
of a world answering back
from greater and greater distances.

Roadway

Twenty years here, before
we needed to raise a fence
on the top of this grassy bank
and found stones, stones, stones.

Wherever we tried, the same,
till a shape began to form,
ghostly under the grass –
a roadway – from? to?

One way crosses our stream,
leads nowhere now any more.
The other arches through air,
our yard busy beneath it.

So the grassy bank's an edge
built up to take the weight
of horse-drawn carts, of people
whose minds hold destinations

our present lacks. Their thoughts
explore as ours do, but not
in the same terms. My own
grow lighter, forefeeling changes.

Heron

Her head tilts to our pond,
its sheen among new-grown flags.
Frogs will dive, make rings
as her shadow passes, repasses.

Fragile, those great wings,
ancient before we began.
They know how to seek, turn
on one wing tip, then the other.

She's free of nothing but a past,
a future – held by gravity,
and the pull of distant stars
blotted by this local dawn.

Not free, I know. But the way
she circles looks like a thought
in progress – sensing some danger,
wheeling towards discovery.

Neither giving up nor landing.
Then she slants her head my way
and makes a decision. The roof
of the barn rises up between us.

Grasshoppers

All of a sudden, such numbers.
Each of my steps disturbs them
wave after wave, these flickers
of life, snatching at grass-blades.

Water rests, layer on layer,
pollen dusting the surface:
amber beneath, astir
with echoing threads of light.

One grasshopper missed his aim.
His powerful legs, helpless,
wrinkle the surface tension.
From beneath him, a puff, like moon-dust.

The great diving beetle rises,
grabs him, dives pulse on pulse,
shoves him to drown in a blur
of algae. Leaves him in storage.

I catch my breath. That beetle
knows how to make a living
from the chancy edge of his world.
Sculls off, silvered with air.

Eels

Glasseels, that in open ocean
passed for glints or ripples,
nose into rainflow freshness.
Their gills flush crimson.

Seeking the bright still cup
of our pond, where swallows dip
to drink, newly visible hearts
beat under see-through skin.

Future years upstream will turn
their skins to brown, then gold,
so that mud-shine conceals them,
and the slimy rims of rocks.

Far off, blue ice is diluting
the Gulf Stream. Their final changes,
big eyes, silver skin, starvation,
may not be enough anymore.

Nosing for salt beginnings,
powerful, ready to breed,
to die, they'll retrace the flow,
so long as the flow goes on.

Fallow-deer

They drift, six or seven
silent does, shoaling
from the deep safety of woods
into the last of the sun.

It's the distance that does it: the vague
darkness of a few, the three
white ones clearer, all facing,
step by step, the same way.

Adjusting binoculars brings
an eye, unafraid, ears
flicking, thin legs, a hint
of weight squelching wet grass.

But they seem even more quiet,
more self-contained, as I hold
my breath, imagining theirs,
their feel for the spaces between them.

Most evenings now, I glance up
to an empty edge, while inside me
their flanks brush twigs, their lips
fumble the forest, nip leaves off.

Shetland Ewe

Last night, held by her wool
in the brambles, where forest and farm
overlap, she must have screamed out.
Now it almost seems I heard her.

When I find them, the bones are still
pink at the joints and moist,
but the meat she lived in has gone
with her fine grey fleece.

Save for a single tuft
on her forehead – this white star
I used to tickle – the skull
sits clean as a desert relic.

And the skeleton, night by night,
disarticulates. Bones migrate
to the forest as badgers and foxes
revisit and drag them away.

I find there is comfort in it.
Something to do with the life
that took hers, its toing and froing
out of sight, and out of control.

Lilac

A head of white lilac
between palm and cheek, firm,
weighty, more deep-water cool
than ever I can quite recall.

I feel my lids close. It enters
then, like a kiss, absent
still but longed for, a touch
almost as real as in dream.

It isn't in palm, on cheek,
but through every cell – not a flower
any more but a huge cool
flood through thought's hinterland.

Ah! Then I go on hacking
between stems of lilac, bare
save for pointed small leaves
cupping the tight green clusters.

I hack at the spring briars,
piling prickly strands to one side,
lifting tight-wintering snails
to a frost free shade out of danger.

Spider

Her long forelegs are tapping
for invisible holds in the smooth
whiteness above my bed,
as if any moment she might

lost grip and fall. I fear
she could enter my dreams as a huge
invasion, be wiped away
to a smear like black blood.

Again and again she cramps
as if in panic. No sign
she hasn't died on the journey
across that preyless desert.

But Poincaré could plot
an almost straight line
from where I saw her first
to the corner above my bed.

When she reaches it, she pulls
threads there, that must be her own,
about her – an Orang preparing
for sleep in a web of branches.

Catkins

The catkins have blackened, pollen
all shed, yellowing the table.
I should have dumped them, but wait,
admiring the branches' angles.

And now look, these new leaves
rootless but coming green
out of dark dry twigs!
I'm suddenly filled with catkins,

the catkins I posted my mother
for my birthday, and after her death
found on the table, close
to a note she was writing me.

It's a mystery I've never known,
her sense of a child somewhere.
For my part, I rushed across borders
as if I could make a difference.

But she did that, by the way
my silly catkins were dusting
her table and, slipped among them,
small flowers she taught me to notice.

World

for Myra Schneider

What would we do without world?
We don't even know what we feel,
what we think, till something out there
catches our eye and draws

a response from the darkness inside,
fills it with places to live in –
streams and trees and flowers
with their own ways of being.

And of course not only good things
come. But among them the loved
faces, those eyes within which
other worlds wait to explore us.

There might be a gesture, a word not
spoken, or a word, or a touch
which we shut our eyes to receive.
What was outside may become then

more of self than our cells helplessly
growing or dying or changing.
One world will open to another.
Through echoes. Through transformations.

Moon

for Walt

Nothing of Earth shows
tonight but the tips of the forest
against a bright white moon
almost full, half risen.

When our forebears saw something like this
they must have wondered how light,
such light, could exist in such darkness.
As for us, we know. And our knowledge

tells how the sun whirls us round,
how the planet's exploded side
was rounded off, like this globe
itself, by the rush of gravity.

A fast wind, silently high,
drives cloud across, and the tree-tops
topple. We ourselves seem
to be moving. And we are, we are!

All at once, it is good to stand
unappalled together. To find that to be,
just here, enjoying all this,
is a thing human minds can do.

Nesting

This year the pear-tree has blossomed
in falling snow. Just one night
between the opening of buds
and the crystallization of rain.

But still the blue-tits slip in
and out of their hole, where a branch
broke away. From here, it looks dark
but warm, amongst all that whiteness.

I have watched them do this each spring
as our lives have changed and theirs
seem not to – the way they land
then vanish one after the other,

not having had to decide:
something that runs deeper
than arctic wind has filled
their beaks with makings again.

Hour by hour, how they work,
whether the white that clings
be petals or drops of water
made brittle and sharp by the cold.

The Pear-Tree

It happens when sunset flushes
the hillside. I glance up,
blind to perspective. Our pear-tree
against the light, has cows,

tiny cows, grazing in the gaps
between branches, on a pink
ground, among swifts and swallows.
An immaculate Persian miniature.

Otherworldly natural light.
'Everything holds together'
a painter might say, standing back
from her canvas with lifted brush.

At other times, when the blossom
hums with bees, when fruit
weighs the branches down, when snow
sticks on that old mossy bark,

I love change all the more. Free of waiting,
expecting, straining, and whether
I see it or not, that light will come.
Just real, like good art. A holding.

Hunters' Moon

A hunters' moon, it's called,
because now, in mid-October,
migrating skeins of geese,
back lit, pass within shot.

There's a sort of transhumance too,
though by truck, when the sheep arrive
from higher ground for the winter,
eager for grass still growing.

But swallows are long gone.
The old pear-tree they mobbed
for its cloud of dancing gnats
has let go even its leaves,

and perhaps in our swollen stream
I'll catch sight of a powerful coil,
an eel heading down to the sea
ready for her final journey.

I feel it too, the draw,
awareness shifting from phase
to phase while green logs
spit and crumble in the grate.

The Bird

How its head vibrates, the beak
braced on a song that flows
without hesitation from depths
of time toward depths of time.

Sounds to be lived by. Like feathers
with nothing to choose but keep skin
sheathed, bones able to fly.
Aware, though not self-aware.

I envy that! But at once
a consciousness echoes in mine –
one which discovered self
as miracle, riches of isolation.

What right have I, late come,
not to use words, not cast
phrase after phrase in search
of a world by that gift made strange?

The bird, running through his beak
a long flight-feather, sits
clear of these words – but, for me,
seen partly through if beyond them.

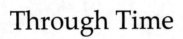

Through Time

At Southerndown

for Tom Sharpe

Melt-water valleys
pour, over these cliffs,
some last signs of ice,
while high
in the sea wind
a falcon strains,
motionless to the eye.

Now, the lit shape
slips, seeking prey,
quivers and again stills –
history
before the ice-age,
before humankind,
astir in that wild skill.

Shifting the shore-line
inland, tides
have prised block from block:
the shock,
as we balance and climb
through this jumbled fall,
to come upon a soft

signature – a small
draped form,
raised, darkening the stone,
a shadow
in the mineral floor
of a dry sea.
We turn for home along the shore.

In the gaps between
fault-lines, pooled sea
rests clear. Anemones,
dark ruby,
cling and feed.
The tide out there,
turning, salts the air.
Swells higher against evening.

Leaving Sully Island

Those round grey stones
unsteadied my feet
as if they could still hold
some pulse from the heavy seas
which broke, rolled,
smoothed them, some vertigo
from vanished cliffs.

The causeway, damp still,
divided the shine,
the silence of slowly rising
waters, a spring tide
coming back in.
I knew I should turn and hurry
but my gaze was held

by delicate pale arabesques
on the stones at my feet.
A million creatures had left
their mark, grazing a green
that my ten-plus lens,
brought close, couldn't detect,
it grew so fine.

This was all beyond my
reach, this flow –
independent ongoing life,
things quite unknown,
unconscious minds
feeding from tide to tide,
doodling grey stone.

At Pantymaes Abandoned Quarry

for David Mitchell

As if, when you tilt the stone,
they had suddenly run
back from our world to their own,
we are left with just
centipede-double tracks,
tiny against the light.
Then, as you move your hand,
these too vanish from sight.

And now you slant it to show
wrinkles in the mud.
Chemical, bacterial? No-one knows.
We are left with just
their shapeliness set to catch
this afternoon's passing light,
a shimmer in the palm of your hand
till you set the slab upright.

And now the edge of the stone
itself has become
movement – as if a flow,
pulse by pulse, nudged
from between your fingers and,
layer by layer, dark, light,
built up this fragment of land
whose pages you turn for our eyes.

Shear-zone at Marloes Albion Sands

So this is where rock
strained on itself
till the layers slid, pleating
where they dragged. Along
each seam are set
scribbles of quartz, its tiny pores
sparkling with held liquid.

Will our water seem precious
to some future eye
(whose mind we can't imagine)
when new rock has risen
veined in white,
the long-ago liquid
of our own world still
unchanged within webs of stone?

At Tredomen Quarry

Through where Britain will be
great mountains rise,
draw from the sky
sweet water, squeeze
Iapetus Ocean dry.
'This took more time
than human beings did
to evolve from the hominids.'

Rueful, we smile at each other,
standing where then,
on land risen
from sea, a river
braided and pooled as it ran.
We gaze down:
something has left at our feet
sinuosities in the silt.

Now turned to stone. A fish-trail.
Bends of a body
pushing itself with fins
and lashing tail.
'From the dentine on its scales
evolved our toothache!'
I notice a flush of saliva.
Did that one reach water?

There comes a waking dream,
we humans lashed
together, black,
sinuous. We seem
to struggle, breathless, overland,
like that fish, stranded –
imperfectly skilled to survive
as the planet warms, dries.

A Graptolite, *Didymograptus murchisoni*

Facing each other
on a wishbone of casements,
your filaments – opal
in the criss-cross glitter
of surface water.

Floating in millions,
filtering the plankton
of a vast ocean
south of the equator,
north of Gondwana.

Our world might not come
from all this, might never
slowly break up
this land, obstruct
the flow of these currents.

All the same, I hold –
where continents clashed –
your saw-toothed ghost
scribbled in a stone
deep-sea black.

Nothing now drifts
where you lived but atoms,
hard and heavy
on my flesh. I'm thinking
life, not extinctions.

At the Glacier's Snout

Sarn Helen, in the Brecon Beacons

Those clouds are sunlit tips
of snow, an ice-age ghost.
Almost invisible, larks
celebrate the present
while we walk up the long rim
at the glacier's snout.

Others walked up this rim
till it became a road.
Real, out-of-reach presences.
Their eyes shadow
our own. Lake-water brims
where the grass grows.

Under foot, the road reverts
to heather, rushes, gorse.
Hunter-gatherers, Celts,
Romans – all
saw something of this, their thoughts
maybe no more

than ours willing or able
to tell the future – ice
become sea, sea become plain,
'this sceptered isle'
made and again unmade.
Lands part, collide.

At my foot I notice a whiteness –
little-finger-tip inner half
of a hatched shell. Out of this,
a mode of life
older than ours. All about us
futures becoming past.

We stand at the dizzying edge.
These temporary hills.
This ancient protected sedge.
In my hand the shell's
light, strong. And somewhere
I hope its bird sings.

Tiktaalik roseae, the Walking Fish

Take away grass from the land,
flowers too, and trees,
so that we're back
with dull earth, shining sea,
little more,
and of what we
most delight in, almost nothing at all.

As now, though, life
was inventing a future:
from under ice
fish that walked on their arms underwater
come to hands
(these gripping fingers)
that have grown from their bones, from fins almost ready to land.

A scuttle in the green skim
at a rivulet's edge,
the prey shadowy
in floating meniscus sky. O then,
the stare
of that gaping head!
That flailing tail. Those elbows. Perspectives of air.

Blackpool Valley, Forest of Dean

In the living forest we seek
signs of buckled layers,
eroded edges, a sea
pinched out of existence
as lands piled up together
slewing north. There's
little sense that Britain is still
moving. We walk up the valley
(old railway cutting), for us a simmer
and sway of leaves, through a day
at ease between sun and shade –
though, in this tangled bracken, webs
affect me like frosted breath
of the forest under our feet,
its cold dark seams.

Elbow-high in growth, we pick
a path to the quarry face.
Friable black, between solid
sandstone, flakes off
in our fingers. *Coleford High Delf.*
A dead source of flame.
And here an adder, suddenly,
makes us stand back, its thin
young inches flashing from sun to safety. We laugh.
Death has come nearer, though.
Tree-ghosted, big grey stones
at the quarry base show matching marks
of fibre, concave and convex.
I have to imagine ghostlier
contacts: ancestors
whose palms may have leant there.

Near the Farmers Arms, Llandegfedd

for Patrick Barkham

Young friesians huddle
in lushness of new pasture –
another farm given up
to yearly stock, its herd of cows,
bred through a lifetime, scattered?
Not to be seen swinging past the town's
bungalow windows, an hour or two before dusk.

But it's time deeper
than that we're after (looking back
as if looking forward): layer
on layer of Silurian siltstone,
pock-marked, shell-packed,
here, in a cutting, out of the sun,
a small dark copse muffling the tock of hammers.

In stony dough
sugared with mica, a hinge –
translucent still, just so,
as it fell, with its pleats
closed against further change,
the rest, the flesh, with seas
that rolled here (above our heads) gone in the flow.

Above desert green
of pasture, a narrow crest
stretches in sun, too steep,
though part of the field, to be ploughed.
Short mountain grass has vetch,
thistle, clover and – down
to where improvement took hold – a sheen of hawkweed.

All this long, hot,
mid-August afternoon
I stay by myself to watch
a hatching of Clouded Yellows.
They shimmer horizon's blue.
With binoculars, I follow,
try to, the vehement zig-zag of wings, not

for more than a moment
folded to feed on the yellow
tassels. And yet, by winter,
all will be dead. I stand
to get closer but, when I do, grow
dizzy as one, silver sun-flash,
white and black dots, molten, whirls in too near.

Up Gwrellech Stream

A dark spring day,
the stream goose-pimpled by rain,
brambles snagging our feet.
All this and our presence itself
scarcely a smudge
on rocks in the making here,
shelf on shelf –
only our minds aware
that this land is travelling slowly north beneath us.

Together we walk on.
Over seas that are now rock.
Over mountains that once were deserts.
Over sands that rivers washed down
from distant peaks
to make a now vanished shore.
It seems that 'now',
the word itself, becomes more and more
strange to us with every step up the stream.

But something catches the eye.
Set askew on the bank, it shines,
wet with rain, so smooth
we can't help running our hands
over its brightness.
Ripples of a river-bed.
Fossilised sand.
Transparencies fill my head –
huge dragonfly wings – and the sky turns bluer.

That was 'now' then:
clear water, a bend
where pulses of sand sparkle
a moment before they fall.
Here now the rain
turns to hail, but a butterfly
dodges it all
with new-hatched wings and hides –
haphazardly, it seems – in the rest of its day.

On the Beach, Ogmore-By-Sea

Seas, settled to slabs.

I pull off a glove
and slip my hand
into a gap.
My fingers move,
tip by tip, over stone.

Runways. Rucks. Burrows.

Braille of what bred us
reading its own
present – the shallows,
the soft mud,
flowing tropical light.

A surface of past life.

Sharp, now, to touch.
Below me, the shine
of our own live
sea, and above,
unique, our surface earth.

Unrepeatable state of the world.

A winter sea, rolling
slowly higher, blurs
with its brilliance, the figures
walking, running, standing
on this long strip of sand.

Cliffs trickle from my hand.

On the Pembrokeshire Coastal Path

A long edge sloping down
to a ha-ha of cliff.
The sea's round brow
motionless, massive.

We watch for whales
as one might watch a brain
for thoughts that refuse to surface.
Uneasy wind, in swathes
of light, of dark,
runs with or against
currents that slowly pass
through the layered cold beneath:
whatever traverses that deep
pursues its way unseen.

Absence remains with me now
as we trudge through pinks
on the narrow path that somehow
clings to these cliffs.

Now and then, at a break
in mounds of colour, my gaze
falls vertiginous, slips
down into seething waves,
the roots of our path,
there where rock has been strained
into faulted loops: the past
still tensed beneath us and we,
somehow, from vanished seas,
emerging to walk and see.

Pillow Lava on Anglesey

Bathers are blurred or distinct,
as wave-flashes
roll the light up
or let it flatten
again and again, *shush*,
shush, stroking the pale
long sands of the bay
into existence, into submission,
Snowdon a mirage
above this airy flow,
magma below
nudging at the scar.

While we made our way through pines,
their dry
darkness, the sand
exhaustingly deep,
no, I couldn't have guessed at
this other world, too luminous
to get in focus,
its grain-quartz gleam,
and blown from the core
this bubbled mass, red-heat
frozen by sea,
stranded on the shore.

Leaning her back on the lava,
a woman
shakes out a rug,
calls to her children
till out of the bright sun,
laughing, teasing, each name
tumbles, each face
focuses affection.
See how we come to each other
out of changes we partly know,
mostly don't.
On occasion, sensing them.

Fossils of Light

for Jeremy Hooker

So heavy with time,
these long leaves
turned slowly to stone.
It seems they must have fallen
while still green
through shadowed light,
a camera-click
of wet silt
washing away air, warmth, sound,
sunk into darkness, becoming ground.

Hard it is,
with such a slab
resting cold on my knee,
so hard to believe
(what I know) that
nothing exists
of the past –
no far
real place, like a walkable landscape
distantly framing the human face.

Letter by letter,
word by word,
the poem fails to catch up
even with this, the one
moment of earth
between past and future.
Stone leaves,
live leaves.
There's a pulse that lasts, through change
after change, out of which everything came.

And will come.
The night sky
shines with fossils of light.
As day succeeds night,
light blinds,
the distant suns
vanish.
I will,
all the same, seek to imagine those clouds
of matter, sparking, seeding worlds out.

Clay

In memory of a student scribe,
Mesopotamia c.2070 BC

the living past, the dying present
Edward Thomas

Preface

The Epic of Gilgamesh originated in Mesopotamia (present day Iraq, southeast Turkey, Syria and southwest Iran). Thought to date from before 2000 BC, it has been described as the oldest surviving poem.

It is thought that the *Epic* (necessarily distorted in my account by being robbed of its puns, sophisticated ironies and much of its magical phrasing) was part of a sacred rite performed over the centuries in ancient Mesopotamia. It has survived on clay tablets bearing cuneiform script. Many of these tablets, often inscribed by young men learning the skill of writing, have survived in whole or in part, while the cities in which they were written lie in ruins.

Most of the known tablets have been translated, with a fascinating introduction, by Professor Andrew George, and published as *The Epic of Gilgamesh* (Penguin Classics, 1999). Direct quotations (in italics) are taken from this translation (see Acknowledgements). *Gilgamesh: A Reader*, ed. John Maier (Bolchazy-Carducci Publishers, 1997) proposes a variety of interesting interpretations of the characters and their story.

The *Epic* became important to me when I first read it in my teens, and certain aspects seemed to find an echo in subsequent experiences. Recently, I was moved to learn that my mitochondrial DNA indicates descent from a woman living some 10,000 years ago in the area now described as Syria. It is with the thought of her world that my poem ends - a world before writing in which tales may have been told which later found an echo in one or another written version of the *Epic*.

Clay

The day he presses the stylus
into clay, he's further before Christ
than I am after. Languages
holding the past for us both.

Is he thinking of making his mark,
or of one, Gilgamesh the King,
who gazed from his city walls
only to see in the river
a corpse floating nameless to sea.
From that moment, Gilgamesh pondered
what might be achieved, that his people
might seek to remember his name,
inscribe it on baked brick.

The student follows his text.
It demands that we climb those walls
(long destroyed) and *walk back and forth*
to witness Uruk's foundations,
its well-baked bricks, its temples.

> But what if he knows we'll look down
> on that river (still flowing), our steps
> and our thoughts, like his own, restless?
>
> I see his young hand, ghostly,
> making strokes for the word *life* –
> life that enforces a journey.
> My own, typing the word.

Text upon text upon text.
And thoughts' unwriteable palimpsest.

> For me, the first time, not a river.
> A cinema screen. Were we there
> for Bambi? A cock crowed

or a hero banged on his gong.
That memory's lost. But not
(my father shielding my eyes
too late) how bodies, naked,
flopped open, scooped in a heap
into that ditch.
                    So later
the sun seemed too bright. I refused
his hand as we crossed the street.

Migrant, I would earn my life.

In the time of the first cities –
as if they knew that our kind
has grown, like all life, from the ground –
they imagined a pinch of clay
becoming a man: wild beast
covered in hair, with tresses
as if both a man and a woman.
At home with gazelles. Eating grass.
Drinking, at dawn, from the water-hole.

Scribed with *Enkidu*, the clay
of the student's tablet takes on
a new echo – flesh too takes on
keener life as a source of words.

Cornelius Lanczos, with Einstein,
had worked on the maths of space-time.
One day, we arranged to meet
in The Institute for Advanced Studies.
He was late. I waited alone.

There were wide-open windows, cases
of books, glass-fronted, locked,
and a table filling the room.
I had time to think of his work -
which he'd helped me, almost, to grasp -
and his own keen grasp of poetry.

Then a swallow flew in, shining,
blue, the sky in its wings.
At risk of a ricochet
from glass to glass.
                    When Lanczos
opened the door, I was up
on the table, barefoot. One look.
Not a word. Off came his shoes.

Side by side, we guided the swallow
out through those windows and back
to the midges and leaves of the Liffey.

My world his world, after all.
A life we could share without words.

His tracks are found by the water-hole.
Had they seen such fossilised footprints
as we have? Pre-human beings,
crossing terrible waterless plains?
Like Enkidu, *Offspring of silence.*

        No language. No clothes. No country.
        Human, yet not quite human,
        a family seeking survival.
        Ahead: unknown hills. Behind:
        their home, enveloped in fire.

When I see a mere butterfly
setting out over open ocean
I think of him, of her,
of the child criss-crossing their trail.
No city ahead. No city
behind. But our future within them,
at risk from volcanic ash
filling (preserving) their footprints.

To us, this would seem a disaster.
They kept straight on. Not running.
Not giving up. Together.

Fearing death, Gilgamesh the King
seeks personal power. He rapes
both the brides and the young men.
No doubt such a king existed:
Shepherd of Uruk-the-Sheepfold!

But how shall we read the Shadow
gods had created for him?
Golden Enkidu, naked,
stinking of the wild, erect
seven days in the harlot's body,
while she does what a woman does
for a man, to help him be human.

Ironic old metaphors!

The student has smoothed his tablet.
He comes to the dream: a rock
drops like a star from the sky.
Gilgamesh struggles to lift it.
His mother, a goddess, interprets:
This rock, it will often save you.
Like a wife, you will love and embrace it.

The men of the kingdom stand by.
He will couple with the wife-to-be.
He first…the bridegroom after.

Unopposed, the king strides forward
to rend the veil. But what's this?
Enkidu, the rock, the star,
stands in his way, pale with anger.

The king, tall and beautiful,
Enkidu, bigger of bone.
But alike as twins. They wrestle.
The crowd is milling about them.
Door-jams and walls shudder.

Till Gilgamesh kneels, *one foot
on the ground.* Each has won the other.

You won me. Your lifelong absence
has drawn me always forward.
The gift more than the loss.
You were my other self.
One I could never be.

In our student days you played Bach,
the Double Violin Concerto –
silence shaped between voices.
Fifty years later your voice
confirmed the unwritten tones
in a printed poem of mine.

Now, you move on before me
into the silence. Your letters
intermittently play their old game
with phrases both odd and right.
But gaps in your thought cause gaps
in your beautiful script. Your hand
may not know my address much longer.

Their legends included a Flood.
At the *glimmer of brightening dawn
all that was bright…turned to darkness.*
Curved horizons, empty of land.

One boat, holding silver and gold,
beasts of the field, man and woman,
aground on a peak. A dove
and a swallow fly far but return.
All the people have turned to clay.
The dead *like fish…fill the ocean.*
A raven finds food, stays away.

First swallow this year. So small,
so sharp in the sunlight, so svelte,
every wing-beat rejoicing to be
here, here again, home once more.

I write where she used to build
before we built. She would swoop
with gobbets of clay to that corner
above where we lie together.

She journeys here still, to our home.
But the planet's heart has erupted
through ice, far to the North.
Like blood roiling through water,
but black, it is coating the light.
Filters down vast horizons.

She got here safely, but now
across Europe the planes are grounded.
Is the breath of swallows clogged
with the sand, the grit and the glass?

Crossing our yard, I notice
again and again how she perches
on a stanchion beside the barn door,
so silent, still on her own.
Not as usual kissing the air.

When I roamed here and there with the herd
says Enkidu, *I knew him,* the Guardian
of Cedars; when axes threaten,
the cedars murmur; he hears them.
His breath is death, his voice
destroys like a terrible flood.

But Gilgamesh disdains the warning.
My friend, you talk as if death
might not come if we stay here, safe
behind the walls of my city.
But I have seen death. I know it.

My hope is to journey beyond
what I know, what I understand,
and *face a battle I know not.*
Leave here *a name eternal.*

And what is the student thinking?
His text is nudging my language.
On an empty well-smoothed surface
his hand is poised to inscribe
what were once someone else's thoughts.

They tell of roads not known,
of a journey unwisely taken,
of sacred groves laid to waste,
their trees felled and made use of -
gates for a great city.

They imagined the goddess Ishtar
leading down the great Bull of Heaven
to dry up *the woods, the reed-beds,*
and marshes, to drain the Euphrates.
His snorts blast gaps in the ground,
where men are lost in their hundreds.

What droughts and floods have we caused?
Is Gaia threading the nose-ring?

The gods have condemned Enkidu.
He will die not as a hero
but helpless. The days are past
when he ran with gazelles. Became man.
Equalled a king in strength.
Undertook the quest for the cedars.

His heroic deeds, after all,
not what the gods had hoped for.

How ancient the work of the farrier,
fitting iron to a wild hoof.

Breaking off, he straightens to ease
his back, remarks he's been watching
a series on the Solar System –
ours, that is…and the suns
of the galaxy, ours…then those others
flung out like grain, their shapes
so various, so far apart.
He smiles: How small we are!

One hand runs strong and gentle
down the feathered leg, which lifts,
gently, to help his reach
as the shoe burns tight to the hoof.

Day after day, Gilgamesh
sits by Enkidu. He mourns
his friend, born of the wild,
suckled by beasts, the friend
once able to run with gazelles.

May the crowd who gave us their blessings,
may the peaks of the mountains *mourn you.*
Can a voice reach him still? *O Enkidu.*
Enkidu. Enkidu. Enkidu.

But the head doesn't lift nor the hand
on that heart sense a sudden beat.

I sat by my mother's corpse.
Her face was grey, stony,
her hand cold. Yet it seemed
her eyes were about to open.

He's unable to bury his friend
till a maggot drops from the nose.

By Enkidu's corpse, Gilgamesh
knows death more closely. No name
on a brick will do now. He sets out
to find life itself. He tears off
his royal robes. He puts on
the skins of wild beasts, such as once
Enkidu had worn in the wild.

> As if through water, a girl
> in a moth-holed jersey – the holes
> my mother embroidered with flowers –
> holds out both her hands to me.
> But I've nothing I feel she needs.
> I find myself stretching out
> my hands, till our fingers meet.
> She steps toward me, she steps
> right into me, out of sight.

Before he leaves, he gives orders.
What is that instinct, to turn
a body to gems, precious metals,
the beauty of alabaster?

> Of phrases too, as in prayer
> or the passing breath of a poem?

> By my mother's corpse I had felt,
> at long last, no terror of death.
> Nothing more precious could die.

Enkidu…has turned to clay.
The student bends to his task.
In clay, he inscribes those words.
Before life began, he was not.
After death, it will be no worse.
Each moment equally real.

For Gilgamesh *the darkness was dense.*
On this journey, nothing behind
or ahead. Just the deepest deep.

Then, all at once, *there was brilliance.*
A cornelian tree was in fruit,
hung with bunches of grapes. Lapis lazuli
fruit-trees, *the trees of the gods.*
Lovely to look on, to touch.

> A poet in our Civil War,
> naked, slept in coarse cloth.
> Woke to his body marked
> with hieroglyphs. Saw his skin
> as a page in an ancient book.
> Not in his own language.
> Living must somehow translate it.
> Too real for words, the silence
> takes shape in a change of heart.

This is the world's edge,
to which Gilgamesh has come.
No longer a king. A wild man,
seeking *the hidden road*
over life's darkest sea.

> If the student stands on the shore
> what does he see? There are oars
> and sails, but no sky-line tankers.
> His sky is possessed by birds.
> His world's not made, as ours is,
> of beings transformed from sea
> to land and from land to sea.
> The monsters he thinks of, out there,
> aren't mammals like giant fish,
> don't sing evanescent songs
> to find their way through the deep.
> His continents aren't adrift,
> his sun, the giver of life,
> not also his planet's doom,
> his space not entwining with time
> and his galaxies, hidden in blue,
> not rushing slowly apart
> to empty the darkness of light.

I have filled my sinews with sorrow
says Gilgamesh. His hair is matted,
the skins on his back are soiled.
And now, while praying for life,
he falls among jewels. He sleeps.

The two who survived the Flood
pity this being, too weak
to watch for long in their world.
Life, for him, waits elsewhere.

The wife kneads flour. Each day
she lays a loaf down beside him.
When he wakes, the dry, the tough,
the soggy, the grey, the mouldy,
they are all there! And the seventh
browns on the coals as he wakes.
It proves how long he has slept.
But also, how good life can be.

Now the skins are thrown to the ground.
The hair's washed clean. The body,
innocent flesh still youthful,
gleams in a life-giving flood –
fresh water, though bound for the deep.

    A storm-wind breathes in the branches.
    Dusk. A man on a horse.
    Its hooves ring on the road.
    The rains begin. Dying sun.
    A chapel set in the woods.
    Shadows in waves on the walls.
    Noises of battle ahead.

    The man is armed and expected.
    But dismounting, he pushes the door.
    Such darkness. Stillness. A cross.
    Where hangs the man who is God.
    A story known all his life.

He kneels. The night sets in.

At dawn, the war-horse is turned
to a road not known – unforeseen
when his master took up the reins.

Turning back from his quest, Gilgamesh
retains one hope: to discover,
in the deepest depths a plant
prickly as coral, the herb
of life-long youthfulness.

Should the old of Uruk taste one leaf,
his return will be welcome indeed!

He steps from his kingly robes
once more. Naked, he dives
down and down till the sun's light fails.
Bursting for breath, he forces
his fingers deep in the sludge.
Nothing, at first, seems alive.
Then they strike the pricks and they grip.

Back above water, he lies
to dry in the sun. And yes,
the hand with the fabled plant
relaxes. He's fallen asleep.
Yet again, he's fallen asleep!
Waking, he's just in time
to witness a snake, the sweet herb
in its fangs, plunge back in the pool.

Grey scales – a transparent coil –
float away from its jewelled skin.

On the shore, his robes await him.

Great libraries ruined long since.
Clay tablets broken. The bones
of hands that inscribed them scattered.

But haunting my thoughts: a poet
whose poems have never been read,
could not even be written down.
His friend, who survived, remembers
how he would mutter, perfecting
each line, while they laboured together
or lay through long nights never sure
to witness another dawn.

Looking up from his task, the student
smiles. Tomorrow perhaps
he'll be set to transcribe more poems
in a language few can still speak,
or to copy accounts, calculations.
But, for now, he is free to go.
The streets of his home await him,
concerns and loves of his day.

    The barley seethes in the sun.
    A woman, a young woman,
    dissolves in the distance, a child
    on her hip, a basket of grain
    on her capable arm. Her senses
    in this, the eternal present.

    In my flesh, there's the evidence
    of her being. Her living trace
    helps hold this pen. But for her
    there's no way of teaching the earth,
    or its fibres, to hold her thought.

    While she turns for home, the Euphrates,
    the river's shadow, is seeping
    through clay deep under her feet,
    plumping the grain, and our present
    (whatever the troubles she has)
    will at most be a flicker of dread.

Ten thousand years in our future
is anyone holding the pen?

And yet, to what stories she listens
round the fire, while her children sleep!

As a wind or an echo rebounds

Plato, *Phaedrus*.

A bright light, already like flame.
Our flowers, hers and mine,
the yellow and the blue of spring,
shut slowly away, going with you.

No words, at least. Only the struggle
of sound against silence, of sound
gradually bringing about its own end.
I'm listening alone now – the shape of your mind
overwhelmingly with me, you gone for ever.

Over her shoulder, in the doorway,
your wife tells me what I need to know,
that my flowers were there with hers by right.
And this message comes also, somehow, from you.

She drives with me through city traffic
like someone climbing a mountain-side,
each hand and foot-hold sure, but jerky,
the same reckless assurance in her parting kiss.
I know, by this, how lucky you were.

Through the train window,
the moon was a cupped hand
held up into the night.
Tilted back by the weight
of so much emptiness.

These words would be so little,
but that with them I walk
a bit more steadily away from you,
closer to you with every step.

Your ashes might have been scattered among mountains.
But afterwards doesn't matter. I see again
that glass-fronted timetable by the lake,
narrow inferno of lovely light.
You were going to help me loose the butterfly
until we saw, that it had no need.

The spaces are familiar.
I travel among them in my mind,
seeking to find, seeking to be dispersed.
The only way to be with you
is to go where we came from.
But I can't tell you even this.
And must wait as you did
after your loved one died, before we met.

I think how you burnt her letters.
How later, in Europe, flames were to change their meaning.
That you must have chosen them to take you.

     Earth's death not only fire, but extreme cold.
     I try to imagine the sudden slow
     winding of a former life in dust.
     Down to the depths beneath their twilight
     her oceans die. But where cold and heat
     are already too deep to change
     something lives on, out of which we came.

Sitting in memory above the sea,
about us the smell of gorse in flower.
As if I could turn round now,
after so long a friendship,
and your arm will be flung out
across my space – the terror
of love about to flow between us.

     Since your death, I wake every night
     at the same hour – some thought of yours
     able to seek me still,
     the way you used to greet me
     between written messages.

After forty years
of inner conversation
I can't get used to
imagining your silence.
But this is my part in your death.
It must somehow be welcomed.

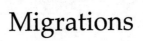

Migrations

A long white edge of land

1939

A long white edge of land
coming slowly up. Something,
more likely someone, made me remember it,
so that even now I can sit again
on my father's shoulder as we come to port.

Since then, coming to land somewhere new
has always thrilled me - the last faint heave,
the see-saw of gang-planks against a quay,
that whole-body cry gulls have, the voices
from shore - above all, their strange intonations.

But these don't remain from that day. Instead,
we seem to be stopped up here in a stillness
more doubtful in meaning than held breath.
The rail gleams under my mother's hand.
No-one, so far, has been getting off.

Bruxelles. Footings of sand

i.m. John Cluysenaar, 1899-1986

Bruxelles. Footings of sand.
In his fingers, a shark's tooth.

While he crouches on broken rock,
time surges over. Like seas.
Vibrations. A taste of blood.
Lost world, sunk in cross-bedding.

His own box of bones, the skull
he looks out from, at once flung open
to forces stretching beyond.

Now his work windows my walls.

Making heads of a changing world.
Making world of the human head.

Edges of canvas no more
than where lines reach in, reach out.

To me, safe on deck, those ships

Goodwin Sands

To me, safe on deck, those ships
seemed to have come from beneath,
from a sea under the sea.

Masts piercing the surface
between different dimensions.

Unknown to me, broken-backed ships,
S.O.S. fires – on sands
made firm by retreating tides
then, as ocean floods back,
fatally quick underfoot.

I supposed world within world
prizing matter apart.

Now, I see helpless men
forewarned by the fate of others
feeling the bank give way.
No ground for last words.

Part of an ancient way

Part of an ancient way,
deep, shaded with hazel,
bending to the right uphill.

We can still stand there,
my mother and I, two ghosts
hand in hand, her eye

for small things giving me
white violets in the damp
green dapple each side of us.

When my memory goes,
so will this, these two
hand in hand nowhere.

I watch her fingers meditate

I watch her fingers meditate
as she puts them aside.
A gesture I never saw.

Did she guess I might keep them,
my two white toddler-sandals,
into old age? I am older now
than she ever became.

Doing my rounds in the barn –
fantails, feral cat, horses –
they've caught my eye once again
in a jumble of things I can't use
but won't chuck away.

As if I could feel a weight
in those tiny feet, my feet –
carrying them to the house –
are feeling themselves responsible
for where we go next.

Late-night London. The Tube

Late-night London. The Tube.
Bright lights. Few travellers. I've read
all the poems in the roof. Far to go.
Tunnels and stations. And tunnels.

Doors again. Open and shut.

Then into me, sudden, a voice
pouring that stranger's language,
flesh to flesh! The woman
passes me by, seeking money
further along, comes back
still singing though empty-handed.

As if singing just for herself
the songs of another country.

It was a round bin, strapped

It was a round bin, strapped
to a lamp-post near Stephen's Green.

Back late from the bona-fide
(too late to slip by the porter
to his student lodgings)
one of us spent the night
sleeping rough, woke to a tramp
making tea and erudite talk.

From then on, we recycled books.
Annotated, wrapped against rain.
Philosophy. Novels. Poems.

Overnight, they'd go from the bin.
Be brought back sometimes
with new remarks in their margins.

The sky is red, hazy, stirring with gulls

The sky is red, hazy, stirring with gulls.
Their cries, their slow shadows, slip by the pane.

We finish our meal. Roof-tops and domes below
dim to a higgledy-piggledy angle and glitter.

All night, without making love, in each other's arms,
we lie on his narrow bed, adrift on friendship.

Out there, the river flows, drawing the air
of inland pastures steadily out to sea.

No, I can't remember his words

No, I can't remember his words,
just the impression left me:
of a young man hurtling zig-zag
through the rush of air, with snow
spurting from under his skis.

A sense of home life awaits him.
Unguessed, is the war ahead.
His escape, on foot, across borders.

Whenever the snows lie deep
on our Welsh hillside, I remember
his memories of snow, passed on
in the language I'm using here
but neither of us were born to.

The track of a fox veers
under wire, trailing spots of blood.
But I won't blot out from my mind
that fenceless mountain: it shimmers
above our snows, while his voice
has survived both words and himself.

Meaning to understand you

Meaning to understand you
I turned from the mantelpiece,
as you had, and spoke aloud
those words you spoke when you left.

I knew you were gone – your footsteps
were still on the stair – but the stance,
the taste, all at once they were with me,
in me, your breath was my own.

I'd invited your heart, left behind,
no matter your words, to draw me
after you - so many years –
and after your death to bring you
back, to warn me in dreams,
again, how painful it would be.

Fossil of its amber forest

Fossil of its amber forest.

Faint as a finger-print,
the seed in its heart would never grow.

But for me the message was rather
how destiny may be folded
on just one particular day
into something, by chance, lasting.

After years at my throat, the drop
broke in two. Amber's memory
had caused the weakness: each half
held a perfect ghostly print.
Where the seed touched both.

Her eyes are green, with ochre

Her eyes are green, with ochre
round the centre – that blackness
through which I am looking at her
and she at me. As once,

bicycling an empty street
at night, I looked down on myself.
Terror of being just there –
knees, body straining, two fists –
then of not getting back inside.

Sometimes alternative words
are like that. Are like this. My hand
trying what I tell it to try.
'I's receding through she after she.

Waiting for tests

The man with the huge hairless head
and a clever slow smile.

The teenage carer who swerves
round a wheelchair, off balance,
and loses the chips from her plate.

And I've noticed a neighbour's mother.
We conspire not to speak, just smile.
So public, all this. So private.

As if in a stained-glass window
a mural of raised wings.
Bright air made of broken mirrors,
where we are reflected. The feathers
blue, red. Distance and flame.

It began with a rabbit bending

for Bonnie Thurston

It began with a rabbit bending
her ears down, to wash them,
on a misty November morning.

While you described her to me
I imagined you stepping closer,
as if you were both in Eden,
neither frightening nor frightened.

It seemed courteous to speak, so you did.
Her answer? To turn a head
with startling signs of survival –
pink skin for eyes, healed over.

So here we were, two humans,
theologian, poet, discussing
a rabbit who certainly lives
with reduced options. But lives.

Ever since, I find myself touched
by three rabbits. A rabbit
greeting the dawn. A rabbit
who must have developed her senses.
A rabbit, for us, metaphorical.

I found myself reckoning up

I found myself reckoning up
how few years remain.

A cloud must have shifted then.
Sunlight on plumes of grass.

On hardly-visible flowers,
three small dark butterflies.

Rain on the opposite hillside
seemed no more than a mist.

But its edge arrives with big
slow drops, then a shower,
and the fluttering wings are gone
among slanting stalks. Their shadows
vanish, as the light dulls.

No depth. Only surfaces.

Put the pen down. Keep looking.
Puzzled that despite awareness
time hasn't yet returned.

As if, eyes open, I'd fallen

As if, eyes open, I'd fallen
asleep. The valley flowed
with shadows of cloud. Far off
a man struck a post, silently.
The *tock* took time to arrive.

Now I can shut my eyes
and know at the least an echo
of whatever had happened when,
not having slept, I woke.

But, to think or express it,
that's not possible. Or needed.
At most, I might say the beyond
was within. No separation.

Had matter turned a gaze
on itself? Seen its own wonder.
Valley still flowing. Man
still striking. The scent of air.

I'll sit by the red valerian

Hummingbird hawkmoth

I'll sit by the red valerian
with my cup of tea. Early evening.

If it comes at all, it will come
punctually, having remembered
this place in summer's geography.

Ah, look! And it's brought another.
They punch the florets. I lean
to the hum of invisible wings.

Inches only between us.

What do their nerve-cells recall
of the waves biting up, salty?

That inkling they must have had
of all this – somewhere else – existing.

Mere canvas – flat, timeless

We live in a rainbow of chaos
                    Paul Cézanne

Mere canvas – flat, timeless.

Contradictions of light betray
hours when he waits between touches.
Pine-needles blurred by nearness
reveal an ache of distance,
bring closer the bulging rockface.

Through his eyes, Mont St. Victoire
thinking itself. And him.

For me, it's the tensions – air
full of that moving light
from far beyond earth.
Thistledown, dragonflies, cloud.

Shapes vibrating between.

Nothing still. Nothing alone.
Co-presences.

Defying syntax.

Soft as water, my finger-tips

Soft as water, my finger-tips
under the salmon's belly,
my elbow braced on grass.
Keeping the mind elsewhere.
Not to let him guess, the way rein
conveys to horse, before fingers
flex, a thought that now
the pace is about to change.

And now, to lift suddenly,
but so smoothly it only seems
a swirl in strong current,
till the air clasps round,
harsh with heat, the floating
surface below him broken,
no water to breathe, nothing
against which to brace his fins.

Glass blocks his pinching and skimming

Glass blocks his pinching and skimming,
solid unflyable air.
What is this change in his world?

He doesn't see when I reach
from the darkness. How could a swallow
turn back now from the light?

As my fingers grip, he fills them
with brilliance. Vibrant sun-warmed
resistance. Indigo pouring.

By a grip that his delicate breast
can breathe in, I've lifted him
to the doorway. His eye steadies.

I watch as he pinches, skims,
becomes again one of many.
I've lost him up there, in the midst.

It will be, I know, some days
before I polish from the window
the print of those pointed wing-beats.

A metaphor for this earth

Tintern Abbey, grisaille

A metaphor for this earth.
Stone transfixed by light.
Letting in green reflections
and the winging shadows.

They gave up the story of Christ
for translucent tracery.

And the stonemasons' skill
preserved, in slim strong mullions,
an orderliness of change,
layer on layer of sediment.

So that now, in this ruin, looking up
from our own thin soil
to empty unbroken arches,
what Cistercians honoured we see –
woods that teach better than books,
the light growth needs.

But suffer the silence too.
Our hum of admiring chatter
taking the place of praise.

I remember this much. The sun

I remember this much. The sun
twisting in knots of cloud
down the glacial cwm, one field
then another lit up like reflections
in running water, as if

somewhere behind my back
a world bent down to look
at itself in ours and vanished
into all this – trees, houses,
black-and-white cows grazing –

and whatever I am had become
awareness only.
                I come to
from this to my usual weight,
the scent of grass, a sea-gull
crying its way inland.

Since then, I'm a wave pulled back
from the sea, separated, delighting
in the eye of light at its centre,
the breaking of spume, but willing
to topple whenever into the tide.

There were dark leaves spread out

There were dark leaves spread out
so that the air between shone
as it narrowed, stretched, shivered.

A bird, never catching its breath,
sang invisibly, not hidden
yet not to be seen by me,

and from the gravel by my foot
a darker-than-red, a crimson
poppy swayed on a thin stalk.

It seemed we were all – tree
and air and bird and poppy and
gravel even - composing together

a secret no one of us
could know, not one escape.
Which breathes itself in us.

They set a great oak upside down

2049 BC

They set a great oak upside down,
as if to grow out of air
into earth. Imagined a future
prepared in the under-world.

They circled to celebrate spring,
summer and autumn, but winter
most of all, when deep out of sight
acorns would come to be shed,
forests begin to unfurl.

In times grimmer than ours.
they dared such a metaphor.

As for me, when the ghost of our oak
hangs in these shallows, unfurling
as if into depths of bright air,
I re-focus my gaze, on mud,
stones, knotted roots
strained by the tree's live weight,
washed bare in the current.

But still, illusions of foliage
silver its flow. Ancestral hopes
reach toward mine. That matter
go on becoming. And becoming thought.